How Clouds Are Made

by Marilyn Greco

PEARSON
Scott
Foresman

DK

What You Already Know

The water cycle is an important part of life on Earth. The Sun makes water on Earth evaporate. Water vapor moves up into the sky. When the water vapor gets cold, it condenses. It changes back into drops of water. The tiny drops of water form clouds. Water falls from the clouds as rain, snow, or hail. It flows into rivers, lakes, and oceans. Then the water cycle begins again.

Weather changes with the seasons. In the spring, the days can be cool or warm. Plants can grow in the spring if there is enough rain.

In summer, the days can be long and sunny. In fall, the days begin to get shorter and cooler. Some animals migrate to warmer places. In winter, the days can be very cold. Some animals hibernate, or sleep, during winter.

Fast-flowing rivers take water back to the sea.

cloudy sky

Wet weather can be dangerous. Lightning, hurricanes, and tornadoes can cause harm. Dry weather can also be dangerous. Too little rain is called a drought. Droughts can harm living things too.

Some scientists watch clouds to understand the weather. Clouds are like clues. They can show what will happen next. Read on to learn how!

Clouds And The Weather

Have you ever looked up at the sky and watched the clouds? What did you see? Did you see a blue sky filled with puffy, white clouds? Did you see a sky that looked dark and gray?

Clouds come in many sizes, shapes, and colors. The sizes, shapes, and colors of clouds are always changing. No two clouds are ever exactly alike.

Just what is a cloud? A cloud is made up of many tiny drops of water stuck together. Clouds float high in the sky.

We can learn a lot by looking at clouds. Clouds can help tell us if the day will be rainy, clear, windy, or stormy. Pay attention to the clouds. Read the information they hold!

Types of Clouds

There are three main shapes of clouds: stratus, cumulus, and cirrus.

Stratus clouds are formed in flat layers. They are low in the sky. When we see stratus clouds, it can mean that a gray and dreary day lies ahead.

stratus

cumulus

Cumulus (KYOO-myoo-luhs) clouds are puffy. They can be gray or white. White cumulus clouds in a bright blue sky often mean fair weather.

Cirrus (SIR-uhs) clouds are thin and wispy. They are high in the sky. Cirrus clouds are made of tiny ice particles. But these clouds almost never make rain or snow.

cirrus

Clouds can be a combination of stratus, cumulus, and cirrus. Scientists give these clouds special names.

The first part of the name usually tells about the cloud's altitude, or how high it is in the sky. The second part tells about its shape. Cloud names that begin with *strato* are low clouds. Those that begin with *alto* are at the middle level of the sky. Clouds names that start with *cirro* are very high.

Stratocumulus clouds are found low in the sky. They are large and puffy. They can make light rain or snow.

stratocumulus   **cumulonimbus**

Cumulonimbus clouds can be thick and dark. *Nimbus* means "cloud." Cumulonimbus clouds bring heavy rain with thunder and lightning, hail, or snow.

Altocumulus clouds are also puffy. They can be gray or white. They are found in the middle level of the sky. When you see these clouds, a thunderstorm may be coming.

Cirrocumulus clouds are fluffy and white. They are formed in strong winds high up in the sky. These clouds can happen when the weather is changing.

altocumulus   cirrocumulus

The Water Cycle

Water moves between the land, the air, and the oceans. It evaporates from lakes, rivers, and plants. It forms clouds. Days later, the water falls back to the land as rain, sleet, snow, or hail. This continuous movement of water is called the water cycle.

2. The warm air rises and cools. Water vapor in the air condenses. It changes into tiny water drops or ice crystals. These form clouds.

1. The Sun warms the water and the air. The water evaporates, or changes, into water vapor.

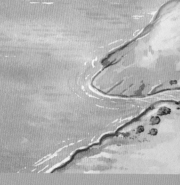

3. The water drops and ice crystals stick together. When they become heavy, they fall to Earth as rain, sleet, hail, or snow.

4. Rivers carry the water back to the oceans.

Making a Cloud

Clouds are a mixture of air, water vapor, and dust.

Warm air and water vapor rise up into the sky. As they rise, they get colder. The water vapor condenses. It turns into millions of tiny water droplets.

1. A small cloud forms.

2. Small clouds gather.

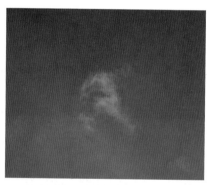

3. Small clouds join together.

4. A large cloud builds up.

The water droplets stick to tiny particles of dust. Many of the droplets stick together to form a small cloud. A small cloud is light. It floats in the sky.

More and more droplets attach to each other. Small clouds join together. Soon a big, heavy cloud is made.

5. Clouds can grow large and heavy. Rain, snow, or hail falls from heavy clouds.

Rain Clouds

Precipitation is the name scientists use for water that falls from clouds. Rain, snow, and hail are kinds of precipitation.

Clouds are made of tiny water droplets. As clouds grow bigger, they get heavier. Soon the drops can no longer float. They fall down to the ground. This is how rain happens.

Rain can be a light drizzle or a steady shower. Rain can be a heavy downpour.

Different kinds of clouds bring different kinds of rain. Cumulonimbus clouds bring heavy rain. Nimbostratus clouds bring light rain.

In North America, we can see rain clouds during every season of the year. However, most rain clouds happen during spring and summer.

Nimbostratus clouds look like a dark blanket across the sky.

Snow and Hail

snow crystal

When the air in a cloud is freezing, water droplets turn into ice crystals. More and more ice crystals stick together. The crystals grow. When the crystals become too heavy to remain in the air, they start to fall.

If the air under the cloud is colder than freezing, the crystals turn into snow. Snowflakes are crystals of ice. Snowflakes can only happen when the weather is cold.

Hailstones can be as small as a pea or as large as a softball!

Hailstones are also made of ice, but they form when the weather is warm. Hail forms during thunderstorms.

A hailstone starts out as a tiny frozen water droplet in a cumulonimbus cloud. Strong winds toss the ice up and down. The ice crashes into other ice crystals and water droplets.

With each toss, another layer of water freezes onto the hailstone. It grows larger and larger. If the wind is strong it can keep tossing the hailstone for a long time. Finally, when the hailstone gets very heavy, it falls to the ground.

Storm Clouds

Thunder and lightning can begin in storm clouds. A storm cloud, such as a cumulonimbus, happens when warm air rises quickly and moves high into the sky. When it meets colder air, the water vapor condenses.

The cloud stops moving upward. It spreads out into a shape that looks like a mushroom. It is wide at the top and narrow at the bottom. At the top of the storm cloud, water droplets turn into ice crystals. They become heavy and start to fall.

Lightning happens in storm clouds such as cumulonimbus.

Ice crystals and water droplets crash into each other. This makes static electricity. The electricity causes bright sparks to light up the sky. This is lightning.

Lightning is very, very hot. The heat from the lightning causes the air to move so fast that it makes a very loud smacking sound. This is thunder.

Fog, Mist, and Dew

Fog, mist, and dew form when water in the air condenses near the ground. Mist is air filled with tiny droplets of water. Being in the mist is like being in a cloud right above the ground. When mist gets very thick, it is called fog. Mist and fog disappear when sunshine heats up the ground and the air. The water droplets evaporate and move higher up into the sky.

Fog is like a low-level cloud.

Dew usually happens at night. Dew forms when air close to the ground cools off quickly. Water vapor in the air condenses into small drops of water. The drops stay on plants and other objects.

dew drops on a spiderweb

Frost may form when the ground temperature is freezing. Dew drops in the air turn into ice crystals. Frost sometimes makes beautiful shapes.

Frost is frozen dew.

Amazing Clouds

Clouds are amazing. They change all the time. They help us know what kind of weather is coming our way. Scientists study the clouds to predict the weather.

Clouds are a part of the water cycle. They form when water vapor in the air condenses. Stratus clouds stretch out in layers. Cumulus clouds bunch together like fluff. Cirrus clouds are high, thin wisps of white. Cumulonimbus storm clouds are shaped like mushrooms.

Scientists name clouds by their shape. They also name them by their altitude.

Are there any clouds today?

Watching clouds can be fun. Dark, gray clouds might mean rain. Fluffy clouds might mean good weather. Next time you are outside, observe the sky carefully. You might be able to predict the weather using the clouds!

Glossary

altitude   how high something is above sea level

attach   to stick to something

continuous   going on all the time

precipitation   water that falls from the sky in the form of rain, snow, sleet, or hail

predict   to tell what will happen in the future

water vapor   water in its gas form